THE SECRET LIFE OF
MOTHMAN

by Megan Cooley Peterson

CAPSTONE PRESS
a capstone imprint

Published by Capstone Press, an imprint of Capstone
1710 Roe Crest Drive, North Mankato, Minnesota 56003
capstonepub.com

Library of Congress Cataloging-in-Publication Data is available on the Library
of Congress website.

ISBN: 9781669003991 (hardcover)
ISBN: 9781669040392 (paperback)
ISBN: 9781669003953 (ebook PDF)

Summary: Readers take a look into the secret life of Mothman to uncover
interesting facts, including the cryptid's flying skills, where it hangs out,
and more.

Editorial Credits
Editor: Abby Huff; Designer: Heidi Thompson; Media Researcher: Jo Miller;
Production Specialist: Tori Abraham

Image Credits
Alamy: Matthew Corrigan, 5; Associated Press: The Herald-Dispatch Archive, 22;
Capstone Press/Matthew Stevens, 21; Shutterstock: buraktumler, 24, Dark Moon
Pictures, 10, DimaSid, 25 (power plant), Djent, Cover (cup), Esteban De Armas,
11, 13, ezp, 8, Flipser, 20, goir, 12, Jack R Perry Photography, 23, JM-MEDIA, 17,
19, ktsdesign, 28, Makkuro GL, 27 (mask), Marcin Perkowski, 25 (bird), Matthew
Corrigan, 7, Olinchuk, 15, PowerLord, 29 (Mothman), Sam of Art, Cover, 1 (skyline),
SimpleB, Cover (Mothman), 9, stockakia, 29 (ball, glasses, umbrella), Sudowoodo,
14 (Mothman), Vldplk, 27 (Mothman), WhirlVFX - Pamela Werrell, 26, zef art, 14
(house)

Design Elements
Shutterstock: vecktor, Kues

All internet sites appearing in back matter were available and accurate when
this book was sent to press.

Printed and bound in China. PO5132

TABLE OF CONTENTS

Words in **bold** are in the glossary.

MEET MOTHMAN

Part man. Part bird. Part moth? Meet Mothman, the superhero of the **cryptid** world. Its super speed put it on the map. It may have even tried to save lives. What else is there to know? Read on about Mothman's secret life.

> **FACT**
> Cryptids are animals some people believe are real. But science has not been able to show that they exist.

MOTHMAN FAN

Mothman's super speed made it famous. How much do you know about this fast-flying cryptid? Can you name its:

1. Height?

2. Wingspan?

3. Favorite time to go out?

4. Hometown?

5. Biggest fear?

ANSWERS

1. 6 to 7 feet

2. 10 feet

3. At night

4. Point Pleasant,
West Virginia

5. Bright lights

WINGING IT

Mothman was named after a tiny bug. But this cryptid has big style. The humanlike **creature** stands on two legs. It's at least 6 feet tall. Huge mothlike wings grow from its back. Reports say it might have feathers.

See a red glow in the dark? It could be Mothman's eyes.

Mothman is one good-looking cryptid!

No one knows how long Mothman has been around. But it's always ready to make friends. Even at a **graveyard**!

Gravediggers first saw Mothman on November 12, 1966, in West Virginia. The men said a brown creature flew from tree to tree. Was the cryptid showing off its flying skills?

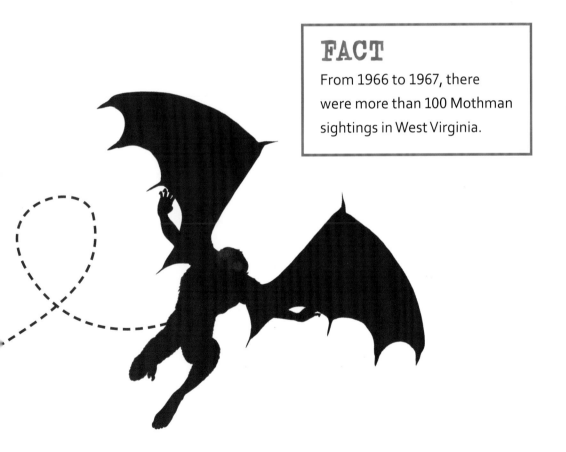

FACT

From 1966 to 1967, there were more than 100 Mothman sightings in West Virginia.

HOME ALONE

Mothman doesn't want roommates. It lives alone in an old weapons factory in Point Pleasant, West Virginia. Miles of tunnels lie below the factory. These tunnels make a great place for Mothman to stretch its wings.

FACT
Locals call Mothman's home the **TNT** Area. The factory made TNT during World War II.

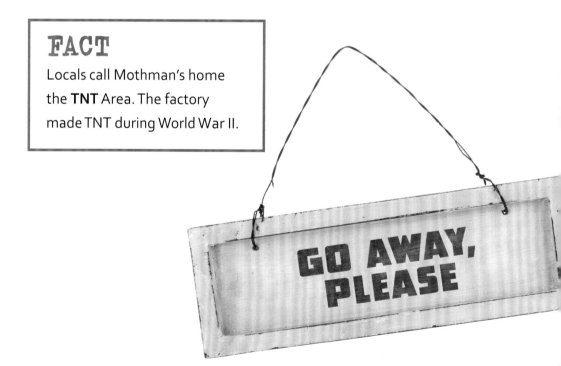

In 1966, a couple who lived near the factory looked out their window. Mothman stood in their driveway. It stared at them. Then it flew away. Maybe Mothman just wanted to meet its neighbors?

SUPER SPEED

No one can beat Mothman in the sky. The cryptid zooms at speeds greater than 100 miles per hour. The peregrine falcon is the world's fastest bird. It tops out at about 80 miles per hour.

But Mothman isn't so great on the ground. **Witnesses** say it trips when it runs.

WANT TO RACE?

Mothman put on a flying show on November 15, 1966. Around midnight, two couples were out driving. They drove near the weapons factory in Point Pleasant. Suddenly, a creature swooped down next to their car. Its flapping wings sounded like a helicopter.

WHOOOSHH!

The couples sped up. Their car raced at more than 100 miles per hour. Mothman kept up easily.

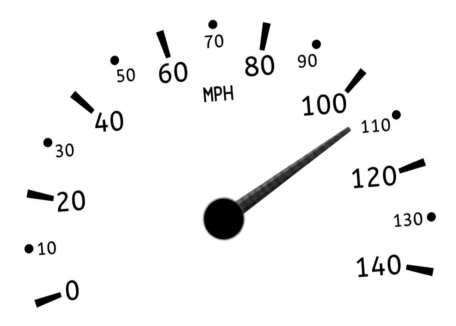

Soon the people drove into town. All the lights spooked Mothman. It flew away. If not for its fear, it would have won that race!

HERO OR VILLAIN?

Is Mothman here to save the day? In 1967, the Silver Bridge fell in Point Pleasant. Mothman had shown up in town a year before. Some think it came to **warn** people. It was trying to tell them something bad would happen. After the **accident**, the cryptid seemed to leave the area.

FACT

Other people believe Mothman caused the Silver Bridge to fall.

BLACK BIRD

Mothman may have flown to Ukraine in 1986. A power plant there blew up that year. Before the accident, workers saw a strange creature. It had wings and glowing red eyes. The workers called it "black bird." Was it Mothman there to warn them?

the power plant

SECRET IDENTITY

Every superhero has a secret identity. So what is Mothman's? Some people think the cryptid might be a large owl or a sandhill crane. Both of these birds have big wings. They can have gray or brown feathers. Sandhill cranes have reddish orange eyes.

We do NOT look like each other! Rude!

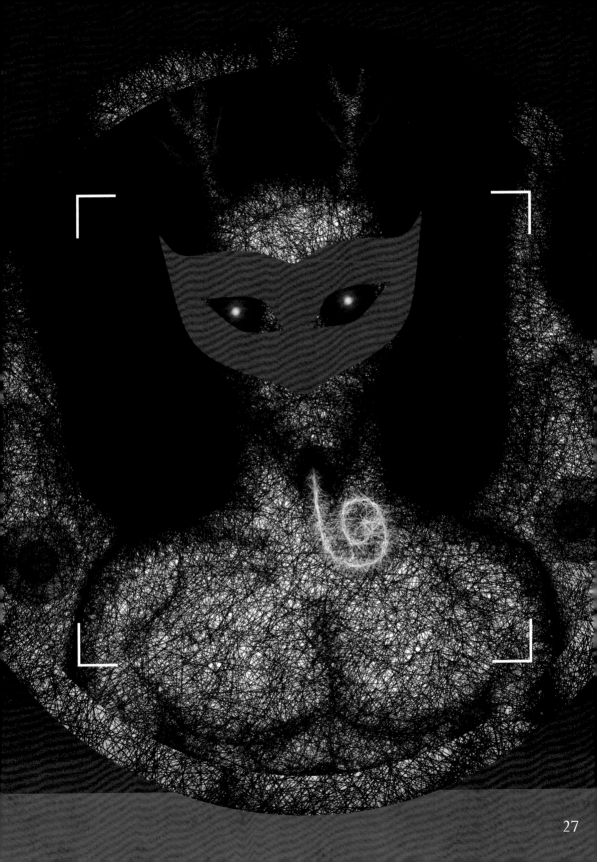

Did Mothman come from another planet? Some say the cryptid is an alien. In the 1960s, many people in Point Pleasant reported **UFOs**. They also saw strange lights in the sky.

Was it Mothman flying a spaceship?

What do you think?

West Virginia? I thought I was landing in Hawaii.

GLOSSARY

accident (AK-suh-duhnt)—a sudden and unexpected event that leads to loss or injury

creature (KREE-chur)—a strange animal

cryptid (KRYP-tid)—an animal that has not been proven to be real by science

graveyard (GREYV-yahrd)—a place where dead people are buried

TNT—a chemical that is used in bombs and other weapons that blow up

UFO—an object in the sky thought to be a spaceship from another planet; UFO is short for Unidentified Flying Object

warn (WORN)—to tell about a danger that might happen in the future

witness (WIT-niss)—a person who has seen or heard something

READ MORE

Bowman, Chris. *The Mothman Sightings.* Minneapolis: Bellwether Media, Inc., 2020.

Finn, Peter. *Do Monsters Exist?* New York: Gareth Stevens Publishing, 2023.

Halls, Kelly Milner. *Cryptid Creatures: A Field Guide.* Seattle: Little Bigfoot, an imprint of Sasquatch Books, 2019.

INTERNET SITES

How Stuff Works: 10 Mythical American Monsters
science.howstuffworks.com/science-vs-myth/strange-creatures/10-mythical-american-monsters.htm

PBS: Mothman: America's Notorious Winged Monster
pbs.org/video/mothman-americas-notorious-winged-monster-ivhuou/

SoftSchools: Mothman Facts
softschools.com/facts/fiction/mothman_facts/2866/

INDEX

ABOUT THE AUTHOR

Megan Cooley Peterson has been an avid reader and writer since she was a little girl. She has written nonfiction children's books about topics ranging from urban legends to gross animal facts. She lives in Minnesota with her husband, daughter, and cuddly kitty.